ι 5.0
P 0.5

AMERICA AT WAR

AMERICA UNDER ATTACK

Scott Marquette

Rourke Publishing LLC
Vero Beach, Florida 32964

Rourke
Publishing LLC

PHOTO CREDITS:
AP/Wide World Photo: cover, pages 8, 10, 18, 20, 25, 30, 32, 34, 36, 41, 42; Defense Visual Information Center: pages 4, 6, 12, 14, 16, 19, 22, 24, 26, 28, 35, 38, 40, 44.

PRODUCED by Lownik Communication Services, Inc. www.lcs-impact.com
DESIGNED by Cunningham Design

Library of Congress Cataloging-in-Publication Data

Marquette, Scott.
  America Under Attack / Scott Marquette.
     v. cm. — (America at war)
  Includes bibliographical references and index.
  Contents: Introduction: "A War to Save Civilization" — Map of Middle East/Central Asia, 2001 — Timeline — Roots of terror — "An Act of War" — A war of many fronts — "The New Normal" — America changed forever.
   ISBN 1-58952-386-5 (hardcover)
   1. September 11 Terrorist Attacks, 2001—Juvenile literature. 2. War on Terrorism, 2001—Juvenile literature. 3. Terrorism—United States—Juvenile literature. 4. United States—Foreign relations—Islamic countries—Juvenile literature. 5. United States—Foreign relations—Middle East—Juvenile literature. [1. September 11 Terrorist Attacks, 2001. 2. War on Terrorism, 2001- 3. Terrorism. 4. United States—Foreign relations—Middle East.] I. Title. II. Series.

HV6432 .M375 2002
973.931—dc21   2002001215

Printed in the USA

Cover Photo:
The south tower of the World Trade Center explodes as a jet slams into it on September 11, 2001.

Table of Contents

On September 11, 2001, the U.S. was attacked by terrorists. A country that thought it was safe was suddenly filled with fear.

Introduction

"A War To Save Civilization"

September 11, 2001 started as a beautiful day in New York City. The sky was sunny and blue. People enjoyed the warm fall day. Then the nightmare began.

With no warning, two hijacked passenger jets crashed into the huge World Trade Center towers. Near Washington, D.C., a jet hit the **Pentagon**. A fourth jet crashed in Pennsylvania. More than 3,000 people died in the attacks.

On that day, a country that had thought it was safe was filled with fear. America was under attack.

Soon there were more reasons for fear. People began to die from **anthrax**. It looked as if the disease was part of a new terror attack. The hunt for the ones who committed the crimes began both at home and in other countries.

After September 11, the U.S. declared war on **terrorism**. President George W. Bush called it "a war to save civilization itself." The war caused a new wave of **patriotic** feeling to sweep the U.S. But it also raised many questions. Those questions would take a long time to answer. Some are still not answered.

The U.S. declared war on terrorism after September 11, 2001.
The war would take U.S. troops to fight in Afghanistan.

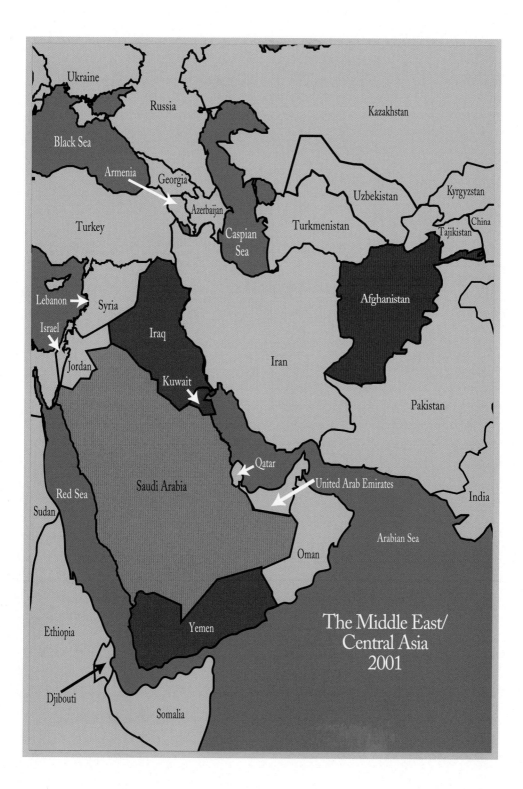

The Middle East/
Central Asia
2001

AMERICA UNDER ATTACK TIMELINE

1988
Osama bin Laden forms al-Qaeda to fight Soviet forces in Afghanistan

1991
January-February: U.S.-led allies defeat Iraq in the Persian Gulf War

1993
February 26: Truck bomb explodes in the parking garage at the World Trade Center

October 3: 18 U.S. Army rangers are killed when they come under fire in Somalia

1998
August 7: Bombs explode outside U.S. embassies in Kenya and Tanzania

August 20: U.S. fires missiles at suspected terrorist sites in Afghanistan and Sudan

2000
October 12: Suicide bombers attack U.S.S. *Cole* in Yemen, killing 17 sailors

2001
September 11: Terrorists hijack four jets. They destroy the World Trade Center and crash into the Pentagon. The fourth plane crashes in Pennsylvania

October 5: Florida editor dies of anthrax inhalation

October 7: U.S. launches military assault on Afghanistan to find bin Laden and punish the Taliban

October 13-19: Workers at NBC, CBS, and the New York *Post* test positive for anthrax

October 15: A letter received at the office of Senate Majority Leader Tom Daschle tests positive for anthrax

October 19: First U.S. ground troops arrive in Afghanistan

October 26: President George W. Bush signs U.S.A. Patriot Act into law

December 7: Kandahar, the last Taliban stronghold, falls to Afghan rebels

Roots of Terror

When the Soviet Union fell in the late 1980s, the **Cold War** came to an end. But the U.S. faced new kinds of enemies. The enemies were not countries. The new enemies were **terrorists**. They formed groups to plan violent acts against the U.S. and other countries. The kind of war they fought was called terrorism. They used homemade bombs or hit-and-run attacks to strike fear into people.

The terrorists were angry about many things. One was the long fight between Israel and the Palestinians. The Palestinians wanted their own nation in the Middle East. But Israel was afraid this country would be a threat. The two sides fought each other for more than 40 years. Terrorist groups like **Hamas** and **Islamic Jihad** were formed to try to make Israel leave Palestine.

In 1991, U.S.-led forces fought the Persian Gulf War. They beat Iraq, which had invaded its neighbor, Kuwait. The U.S. forced **sanctions** on Iraq so it could not trade with other countries. Some felt the sanctions were too hard on the people of Iraq. Others were angry that the U.S. troops that had come to Saudi Arabia to fight the war were still there. They felt Saudi Arabia was holy to the

Osama bin Laden, a wealthy Saudi, formed al-Qaeda to help force the Soviet Union out of Afghanistan. He later planned terrorist acts against the U.S.

religion of **Islam**. They did not like non-Islamic troops staying there.

One of those who were angry was **Osama bin Laden**. He was the son of a rich Saudi family. In the 1980s, he went to Afghanistan to help fight the invading **Soviets**. Bin Laden was a hero in Afghanistan. He formed his own group, called **al-Qaeda**, which means "The Base." He wanted to train fighters to defend Islam.

After the Soviets left Afghanistan, bin Laden turned his sights on the U.S. He wanted to force the U.S. to take its troops out of Saudi Arabia. He

Osama bin Laden

When the Soviets left Afghanistan, Osama bin Laden went home to Saudi Arabia. There he started several businesses. He formed al-Qaeda training camps. But the Saudis made him leave in 1996. He went back to hide in Afghanistan.

also wanted to stop the U.S. from helping Israel in its fight with the Palestinians. He called for a **jihad**, or holy war, against the U.S.

Bin Laden and al-Qaeda soon began to strike. In 1993, a truck bomb blew up in the World Trade Center. Six people died. One of the men who helped

On October 12, 2000, suicide bombers blasted a hole in the U.S.S. Cole, killing 17 sailors.

in the bombing had links to al-Qaeda. That same year, U.S. Army Rangers on patrol in Somalia suddenly came under fierce attack. Eighteen were killed. Some of their attackers were from al-Qaeda.

In August 1998, bombs destroyed two U.S. **embassies** in Africa. The attack killed 250 people. Several of the men arrested for the crime had ties to bin Laden. The U.S. struck back. It fired missiles at al-Qaeda bases in Afghanistan. The bases were damaged. But bin Laden was not stopped.

In October 2000, a small boat drew up to the U.S.S. *Cole*, a navy ship stationed in Yemen. The men in the boat blew up a bomb. They killed themselves and 17 U.S. sailors. The bomb blew a hole in the side of the steel ship. It was thought that the bombers worked with al-Qaeda.

But Osama bin Laden had an even bigger attack in mind. Once more, his target would be the World Trade Center.

Rescue workers desperately searched for survivors in the smoking ruins of the World Trade Center.

"An Act of War"

On September 11, 2001, teams of men hijacked four passenger jets. They were armed only with knives and box cutters, but they took control of the jets. They flew two of the jets into the twin towers of the World Trade Center. A third jet slammed into one side of the Pentagon, the headquarters of the U.S. armed forces, near Washington, D.C.

All of the jets were full of fuel. They blew up with terrific force when they hit. Large fires started. Police and firefighters rushed to the scene. In New York City, those who worked in the World Trade Center tried to flee the burning buildings.

People on the fourth hijacked jet heard the news. They called their loved ones on cell phones and learned of the attacks. Some of the passengers decided not to let their plane be used as a weapon. They risked their lives and fought with the hijackers. The plane crashed, killing all aboard. It was later learned that the hijackers probably meant to crash the jet into the White House, the U.S. Capitol, or Camp David, the president's private retreat.

About an hour after the first attacks, fire began to melt the steel of the World Trade Center. As the world watched in horror, both of the giant,

A hijacked jet slammed into the side of the Pentagon in Washington, D.C., causing massive destruction.

110-story towers crumbled to the ground. Thousands of people in and around the buildings, including rescue workers, died in an instant.

The stunned nation quickly acted to protect itself. President Bush, who was in Florida, was whisked away to safety. For the first time since the War of 1812, the White House was **evacuated**. Other government buildings were also emptied. Fearing more attacks, the U.S. told all jets in the air to land at once. It ordered no planes to fly.

Around the world, people reacted to the attacks. Tall buildings and government centers were emptied. Stock markets were closed. Armies were called on alert. Leaders spoke of their anger and shock at the attacks. People everywhere stopped what they were doing to watch the scenes of destruction on television.

President Bush returned to Washington that night. He spoke to the world on television. He

A Different Kind of War

President Bush told the American people that the war on terrorism would be a different kind of war. It would be fought with legal and financial weapons as well as military ones. Some of it would be fought in secret. And he warned it would not end soon.

Americans were shocked and afraid when they learned of the terrorist attacks on September 11.

called for people to pray. He vowed that the U.S. would strike back at those who had planned the attacks. He said the U.S. would also punish countries that helped the attackers.

The **FBI** immediately began the hunt for those who helped in the attacks. What they found out was shocking. The 19 hijackers were from Saudi Arabia and other countries in the Middle East. Some had lived legally in the U.S. for more than a year before the attack. Some even learned to fly jets at U.S. flight schools. Two of the hijackers had been on an FBI "watch list" because of their ties to bin Laden and the U.S.S. *Cole* bombing.

The fires at the World Trade Center burned for weeks after the attack. No survivors were found in the ruins.

While many people across the world condemned the terrorist attacks, some protested in favor of Osama bin Laden.

President Bush declared a war on terrorism. He asked other countries to help the U.S. bring terrorists to justice. He said the U.S. could prove Osama bin Laden was behind the attacks. Bush called on the leaders of Afghanistan to turn over bin Laden and the rest of his al-Qaeda network. But the **Taliban**, who ruled Afghanistan with their own harsh kind of Islam, refused. Bin Laden had helped them get control of the country and they would not give him up.

A war of words started between the U.S. and the Taliban. But that war would soon turn deadly.

On October 7, 2001, the U.S. launched strikes against al-Qaeda and Taliban forces in Afghanistan.

A War of Many Fronts

In the old way of war, a **front** was a place where armies fought. A country might have to fight on one or two fronts at the same time. But the war on terrorism is a war of many fronts. It is fought by police, diplomats, lawyers, bankers, and spies as well as by troops.

The first military front opened on October 7, 2001. President Bush ordered U.S. planes and missiles to strike Afghan targets. The strikes were to punish the Taliban for helping bin Laden. They were also meant to crush al-Qaeda. Bush hoped to kill or catch bin Laden.

George W. Bush

President Bush is the son of George H.W. Bush, who was president from 1989 to 1992. The senior Bush led the world in the war with Iraq. His son has said that Iraq could be another target in the war on terror.

Even as Bush announced the strikes, a tape of bin Laden was played on TV. In the tape, he praised

U.S. troops fought alongside Afghan resistance fighters to drive the Taliban and al-Qaeda out of Afghanistan.

the September 11 attacks. In this and later tapes, bin Laden seemed to say he was behind the attacks on the U.S.

Most of the U.S. strikes came by air. The U.S. sent some troops into Afghanistan. But Afghan rebels who opposed the Taliban did most of the fighting on the ground. With the Taliban made

*Attorney General John Ashcroft asked Congress for broad new
powers to capture suspected terrorists in the U.S.*

weak by U.S. bombs, the rebels took town after
town. By mid November, the rebels held Kabul, the
Afghan capital. On December 7, they took Kandahar,
the last big city held by the Taliban.

The rebels then turned to fight al-Qaeda. They
fought a fierce battle at the al-Qaeda base at Tora
Bora. The U.S. helped with huge bombs that

President George W. Bush thanks firefighters and other rescue workers who saved lives on September 11.

destroyed the caves where al-Qaeda troops hid. By late December, most of bin Laden's men were dead or on the run. But no one knew where to find bin Laden.

The war on terrorism was also fought on the legal front. Around the world, terrorist suspects were tracked down. People with links to al-Qaeda were caught in many countries. The U.S. held more than 1,000 people it thought might know about terrorists.

U.S. Attorney General John Ashcroft said he had to have more tools to stop terrorism. In October, Congress passed the U.S.A. Patriot Act. The law gave the U.S. more power to listen in on phone calls. It also let the government hold foreign terror suspects for a long time without charging them with a crime. Some people were glad the law was passed so fast. But some feared it gave the U.S. too much power to spy on people and hold them in secret.

Other moves on the legal front were also questioned. President Bush signed an order that said some terrorist suspects might not be tried in regular courts. Instead, they would be tried by **military tribunals**. These courts would be secret. They gave the defendants fewer rights. Bush said the tribunals were needed for swift justice. But many people felt that the president was trying to

A member of Afghanistan's Northern Alliance checks his ammunition. These rebel fighters helped drive the Taliban and al-Qaeda forces out of their country.

get around the court system. They feared the rule would deny suspects their rights.

The war was fought on other fronts, too. Bush seized the funds of groups that helped terrorists. The U.S. shared secret **intelligence** information with other countries, hoping to track down terrorists. There was also a **diplomatic** front. Secretary of State Colin Powell went to many countries. He asked countries like Russia and Iran to work with the U.S. to fight terror.

One month after the first strikes on the U.S., a deadly new front opened. It was a battle against a new, unseen enemy.

New security measures at airports caused long lines.

"The New Normal"

In the wake of the September 11 attacks, life changed in America. New security rules meant people were searched as they went in public buildings. Major sports events and shows were cancelled. People feared that crowds would be targets for terrorists. At baseball's World Series, planes were stopped from flying over the field.

Leaders asked people to be more careful and alert. At the same time, they told people not to be afraid, to go back to a normal life. But no one knew what "normal" meant in this new world. No one was sure where the next strike would come. Guards were sent to government buildings, nuclear plants, fuel plants, and other places that could be targets.

The U.S. economy was hit hard by the attacks. Planes

Waiting in Line

The biggest changes came at airports. People had their bodies and their bags searched. The new security rules caused long lines and delays at airports. Some people decided not to fly at all.

National Guard troops
provided security at the 2002 Winter Olympics
in Salt Lake City, Utah.

could fly again the week after the attacks. But people were afraid to fly. Airlines had fewer customers and higher costs. They laid off thousands of workers. Stock prices fell as investors worried about the future. Soon, workers in other industries lost their jobs, too. The U.S. economy, which was already in a **recession** before September 11, slowed even more.

Some people had to fear their neighbors. **Muslims**, or even people who looked like they might be from the Middle East, faced threats and attacks. Many of these people were citizens who had lived in the U.S. for a long time. President Bush told the country that we were at war with terror, not with Islam. He asked people to reach out to their Muslim neighbors and not to blame them.

In October, a new, real cause for fear emerged. An editor for a national magazine died of anthrax. Anthrax is a disease that normally strikes cows and sheep. But it can be used as a terrorist weapon, too. When anthrax spores touch the skin, they can cause dark, itchy bumps. But when they are breathed in, they can cause death in a few days. Many countries, including Russia and Iraq, have made anthrax into a weapon.

At first, no one was sure if this was really a terrorist attack. But then letters with anthrax came to the offices of TV networks and newspapers in New York City. A letter with anthrax was found in the office of Senate Majority Leader Tom Daschle. Worse, more people began to die of anthrax. By November, five people had died of the disease, including two postal workers who had handled the letters.

The letters made threats against the U.S. and

A worker in a hazardous materials suit works to clean anthrax from the Hart Senate Office Building in Washington, D.C.

Israel. They talked about the September 11 attacks. Police thought they were the act of a terrorist. But there were no clues to link the letters to bin Laden and al-Qaeda. Police had few leads to use in tracking down the killers.

The anthrax attack caused new waves of fear to spread. People were afraid to open their mail. Tons of letters to the U.S. government were left unopened until they could be checked. People rushed to get drugs to protect themselves from

A hazardous materials specialist looks for biological agents in a sample taken from New York's Yankee Stadium.

anthrax. The Senate Office Building was closed for months as health workers tried to stop the anthrax there. But by the end of the year, the attacks seemed to have stopped.

Despite their fear, Americans gained a new feeling of patriotism after the attacks. Sales of U.S. flags soared. People put signs saying "United We Stand" on their cars and homes. Americans gave

*Many Americans responded to the terrorist attacks
with a new feeling of patriotism.*

millions of dollars to help the victims of the attacks. And they stood in line to give blood for the wounded. Many felt that no matter how bad things got, the country would stay strong.

Most people felt proud of their country and supported the war on terrorism. But many still had questions about the future.

America Changed Forever

As the year 2002 began, the war in Afghanistan seemed to be almost over. But it looked like the war on terror had only just begun.

Most Americans were glad that Osama bin Laden could not use Afghanistan as a terrorist base any more. Many members of al-Qaeda had been killed. Others were caught and would face trial. In the U.S., the court case against the first man to be charged with helping the September 11 attacks got under way.

But bin Laden had still not been found. Some thought he may have been killed in the caves of Tora Bora. Others said he was hiding in Pakistan. The head of the Taliban, Mullah Omar, was still on the loose, too.

As Americans looked to the future of the war on terrorism, they had more questions than answers. Would the defeat of al-Qaeda mean an end to terrorist acts in the U.S. and the rest of the world? Or would bin Laden live to strike again? What about other countries that helped terrorists, like Iraq and Sudan? Would the U.S. send troops to these

In March 2002, U.S. forces fought one of the largest battles against al-Qaeda and the Taliban during Operation Anaconda.

countries too? Would the wars there go as well as they had in Afghanistan?

There were questions about the war at home, too. Who had sent the deadly anthrax letters to the media and Congress? Were more on the way? Would terrorists try once more to hijack planes or blow them up? Would there be other kinds of attacks — attacks with deadly chemicals, or other kinds of diseases, or even **radioactive** materials?

People wondered about how the war on terrorism would affect their own lives. Would they ever feel safe again? Would they ever see the end of long lines at airports and security checks at public buildings? Would things ever go back to the way they were before September 11? Or was this life of worry and caution really the "new normal?"

An image of Osama bin Laden taken from a video broadcast in December 2001. By Spring of 2002, no one was sure if bin Laden was still alive.

Secretary of State Colin Powell traveled to many countries to build support for the war on terrorism.

People had many questions. They worried about what was to come. But they also had a new sense of hope. They saw people and countries working together in ways they never had before. Yes, we had new enemies. But some of our old enemies, like Russia and China, looked like they might now be friends.

Most of all, Americans had a new sense of who they were. They saw the bravery of the police and firefighters. They saw the quick results of U.S. military strength. They saw the patience of those who faced delays and inconvenience. And they saw the generosity of those who gave their money and time to help the victims of terror.

America did feel a new fear. But it was still a great country. And it was worth fighting for.

Colin Powell

Colin Powell's parents came to the U.S. from Jamaica. He first won fame as the head of the U.S. armed services during the Persian Gulf War. Powell was so popular that George W. Bush picked him to be secretary of state even before it was clear Bush would be president.

In the first part of 2002,
American troops were still patrolling Afghanistan
in search of Taliban and al-Qaeda forces.

Further Reading

Edwards, Richard. *International Terrorism*. Rourke, 1998.

Ganeri, Anita. *I Remember Palestine: Why We Left*. Steck-Vaughn, 1994.

Italia, Robert. *After the Storm*. Abdo, 1992.

Kerson, Adrian. *Terror in the Towers: Amazing Stories from the World Trade Center Disaster*. Random House, 1993.

Louis, Nancy. *Osama bin Laden*. Abdo, 2002.

Shields, Charles J. *The World Trade Center Bombing*. Chelsea House, 2001.

Websites to Visit
Attack On America Tuesday 11 September 2001
www.webpan.com/msauers/911/wtc.html

Great Buildings Online: *World Trade Center*
www.greatbuildings.com/buildings/World_Trade_
  Center.html

The Terrorism Research Center
www.terrorism.com

Glossary

al-Qaeda — group formed by Osama bin Laden in 1988 to fight the Soviet Union in Afghanistan and defend Islam

anthrax — a deadly disease that can be used as a terror weapon

Cold War — conflict between the United States and the Soviet Union between 1945 and 1990

diplomatic — use of talks and agreements to solve differences between countries

embassies — nations' formal headquarters in other countries

evacuated — emptied of people, usually in an emergency

FBI — Federal Bureau of Investigation, the branch of the U.S. Justice Department that investigates federal crimes

front — an area where wars are fought

Hamas — a Palestinian group seeking to create a homeland near Israel

intelligence — information, often secret, about a country or group

Islam — one of the three major world religions that believe in one God; founded by the Prophet Muhammad in the 7th century

Islamic Jihad — a terrorist group based in Egypt

jihad — "holy war;" an Islamic concept meaning to struggle or fight for the faith

military tribunals — secret trials held by military officers instead of judges

Muslims — people who follow the religion of Islam

Osama bin Laden — Saudi millionaire, head of the al-Qaeda terrorist network

patriotic — a feeling of pride in one's country

Pentagon — the five-sided headquarters of the U.S. Department of Defense, in Arlington, Virginia, near Washington, D.C.

radioactive — poisonous substances often used to make nuclear weapons

recession — a period of time when the economy is shrinking, sales are low, and jobs are lost

sanctions — rules forced on a country to punish it for some act

Soviets — people from the former Soviet Union

Taliban — rulers of Afghanistan from 1996 to 2001

terrorism — use of violence to strike fear into people

terrorists — people who practice terrorism

Index